You've got to dance like nobody's watchin'

Susanna Clark and

Richard Leigh

For Todd Stanton – with gratitude for giving me the knowledge that I am worth loving

Published in the United Kingdom by

freedomDANCE House
www.freedom-dance.com

A CIP record of this book is available from the British Library.

First printed September 2020

Layout and design by Vladimir Goroshko

ISBN 978–1–9161006–0–2

Contents

Foreword

In February 2017, I said a little prayer, wished myself strength, patience and faith, stepped into the darkness and closed the door behind me. I spent three weeks in a *kuti*, a special structure that has triple walls to seal you off from the rest of the world, as part of an ancient Ayurvedic procedure.

I've been coming to India regularly for traditional rejuvination treatment for well over a decade. And yet, it was the first time I had done something like this! Three weeks in the darkness. Three weeks without normal food: just two kinds of Ayurvedic medicine – 100 g of medicinal jam and 30 ml of medicated oil – and three glasses of warm milk a day. Three weeks of prayer, meditation and reflection on my life so far. There were extended moments of bliss when I physically sensed overwhelming love for so many people and so many things in my life. There were also hours of struggle: grudges and hurts, anger with myself and others, wanting to be somewhere else and soon...

The experience was not supposed to be a physical endurance test (as in "I've managed to stay in darkness with no food for three weeks!"), but primarily a spiritual healing ritual. Traditionally, most of the time in the *kuti* is spent in chanting. My adapted version of this experience included dance. How could it not? Dance has been one of my main spiritual practices and I felt it was the most appropriate thing to do while in the *kuti*. My doctor who had done the ritual elsewhere and then built a *kuti* at his Ayurvedic centre supported my view. So, I danced every day.

I always loved to dance, although I was never particularly good at learning steps, and my joints often got injured when, occasionally in my 20's, I went to dance classes.

My life changed dramatically with the discovery that there was no need for learned steps at all in order to experience the full joy and expression that dancing can give us! All we have to do is commit to our dance as a meditative journey and gradually build up the intensity of our movement, stay for some time at the peak and then let our dance gradually settle.

I loved the simplicity and the power of this kind of dance so much that I began sharing it with others and founded freedomDANCE, a school of dance meditation and conscious movement that today trains teachers and brings together communities of dancers around the world.

In the following text you will see references to the freedomDANCE cycle. This is our main method. It's a dance that consists of three stages. First comes Opening. This is when we 'raise the temperature' and where we discover resources that we need for a deep movement experience: our body, the space that we have, and each other. The second stage is the peak of our journey, and it is called Transformation. This is where everything is mixing and merging: body parts, energies, the past, present and future. Something that is truly ours stays with us, something that we don't need goes, and something new that we are ready to welcome emerges. Finally, when we settle, we experience a deep sense of acceptance – this is Freedom, the third stage – freedom to be ourselves, and to be ourselves not alone but with everyone and everything around us.

I stepped into the *kuti* at a turning point in my life. My longest, happiest and most rewarding relationship was coming to an end. Also, I had just lost my father, my last surviving parent. It was a new situation; I had no one to look after or be with. I also developed a lot of pain and discomfort in my right hip and the surrounding areas. Now I know that it was due to premature osteoarthritis which was caused by an congenital hip dysplasia. Sometimes, I could not sleep at night because of the pain and I could not walk without limping during the day. As I was entering the *kuti* and closing its door behind me, my main question was "What's next?". I was hoping that the three weeks of reflection would show me a direction where I could take my life further.

The dances that happened in the dark were very different from my usual dances. I recorded my reflections on a dictaphone after each dance in the *kuti* and I was fascinated to listen to them later. I am moved to share these reflections with a larger world. I hope that the words that I recorded after dancing and the accompanying images that have been added later give food for imagination and inspire something beautiful and meaningful.

introducing me to Ayurveda. This little book would not have been the same without its illustrations. These were specially created by a wonderful artist, Yuri Vinogradov. Getting to know him and having this creative collaboration has been a true gift. I am deeply grateful to my colleagues and friends: Nina Robertson for editing my English and helping me shape up the material for publication; Lora Romanenko for translation and other support; Julia Chernova and Maxim Shumilov for their ideas about illustrations; Vladimir Goroshko for his impeccable and thoughtful graphic design work; and Di Hinds and Irina Krivoshekova for their helpful feedback on my drafts.

I would also like to acknowledge my wonderful conscious movement teachers, who helped me a great deal to get to where I am: Adam Barley, Andrew Holmes, Andrea Juhan, Anna and Daria Halprin, Bodhi Hunt, Cathy Ryan, Gabrielle Roth, Jonathan Horan, Kathy Altman, Lori Salzman, Sue Rickards and many, many others.

The Dance that Didn't Happen

6 February 2017

(during a trial couple of days in the kuti, done as a preparation for the three weeks of isolation to come)

Shall I dance? I think not. I haven't even recorded anything about yesterday's dance! I was going to dance yesterday but I was so unsure about the space: What? Where? How?

There are days like this – you could call them empty. Yes, I shook my hips a bit, shook my body, massaged myself, and nothing got started! My dance ended before it began.

If I look back and think, of course, I know what I should have done and what should have happened: I needed to do a body scan in movement. And then, maybe, something would have happened. Open the body first and then the space will open to you. Just like that.

So – three weeks of dancing in the dark…

Dance Hall

12 February 2017

(the ‘real thing’, the three continuous weeks in the kuti start here)

The first dance in the darkness has happened! It was short. In essence, I was dancing to the music that was inside me, and eventually the sound came out and I found myself humming.

The dance happened gradually and came from within. I decided to do a body scan and swept quickly from my feet up to my head and then along the arms. I was wearing a *dhoti* (a garment traditionally worn by men in Kerala) and eventually took it off and danced naked. I touched the ‘hedgehog’ of my shaved head from time to time.

I can feel my hip, of course. It doesn’t like it. Well, I can’t say it does not like it… it’s just that the movement causes discomfort to it and, for now, the discomfort doesn’t leave me, so I will use this opportunity to dance even when the hip is complaining.

Overall, I enjoyed it! Next time, I will wait for the last traces of light to disappear and then dance in total darkness.

At least I'd created the infrastructure before I moved in! I'd removed a mat that was here on the floor before. I'd found space. I put two yoga mats in one line – created a long pathway – nine whole steps! I won't get lost even when it's completely dark. It will be cool just crossing this room like this. I wanted to say, 'Crossing the dance hall!' Yes, I can cross my dance hall with my eyes closed, just like I am doing now. I also have a little dance floor. It's a small square where there's nothing at all – maybe three steps by three steps. It's boarded by my bed and a wall. There is a little hazard on the third side – a corner. However, I think I will be all right.

I will be able to use this little dance floor, at least a little, every day. My dance may be just in silence. Or, sometimes it could be to a melody. Like today, a melody just passed through my entire body. And then I started humming it and dancing to my own voice. Or it could be a dance with the sounds that penetrate the walls. Right now, I can hear a rooster and the chirping of the birds.

It's getting darker, but it's not yet completely dark.

What do I mean when I say, ‘complete darkness’ if I am supposed to be in complete darkness all the time? I’ll try to explain. At the height of the day when the sun is shining outside, there is some reflected light coming through the windows into the room. I can see vaguely the outlines of the windows though I still don’t see my own body, or anything else, really. Sometimes, I can make out the white sheets of the bed – *sometimes* – particularly, when I compare what I see in that part of the room with what is immediately next to it: the entrance door that is really black. Looking at that contrast, I can discern the difference during the day time. But if I look at my arms or my belly I can’t see them at all at any time of the day. So it is dark, really dark, always. I realise how everything is relative; that little bit of reflected light makes such a huge difference to me here. Now that even outside is dark, here it is total darkness. And it’s wonderful.

I can see how different it is already though, compared to the height of the day. Everything is moving towards complete darkness. Yes, my plan is to wait for it to arrive next time so that I can dance in the pitch-black darkness. I think it will be different.

Drums

12 February 2017

I can't resist the drums even though I danced already! The drumming usually happens here only once a week, it seems. So, I decide: if not today, I'll have to wait for them for an entire week! I let myself loose in the dance. I am dancing to the sound of the drums. Even though there are three layers of wall and a distance that separate me from them, they really give me the beat – sometimes sharp, sometimes very high and continuous. It's so wonderful for letting go, for shaking.

Shaking is my anchor today. There is even some expression in my dance. If I think of the energy that is present, there is both release through shaking and, as a contrast to this, clarity and definition. I even make use of the path that I have made of the two yoga mats; it helps me walk across the room – my dance hall! As things speed up and grow, the definition is erased and turns into shapelessness, smudginess – in essence it turns into its opposite. Just a moment ago there was clarity and order, and suddenly it's all about utter messiness. Although the same impulse is still alive inside that shaking, it crosses over into a new dance. The shaking movements are smaller, faster and more frequent and directed towards the floor now.

Maybe I'll dance more tonight. Even though I am pressed for time with my recapitulation work…

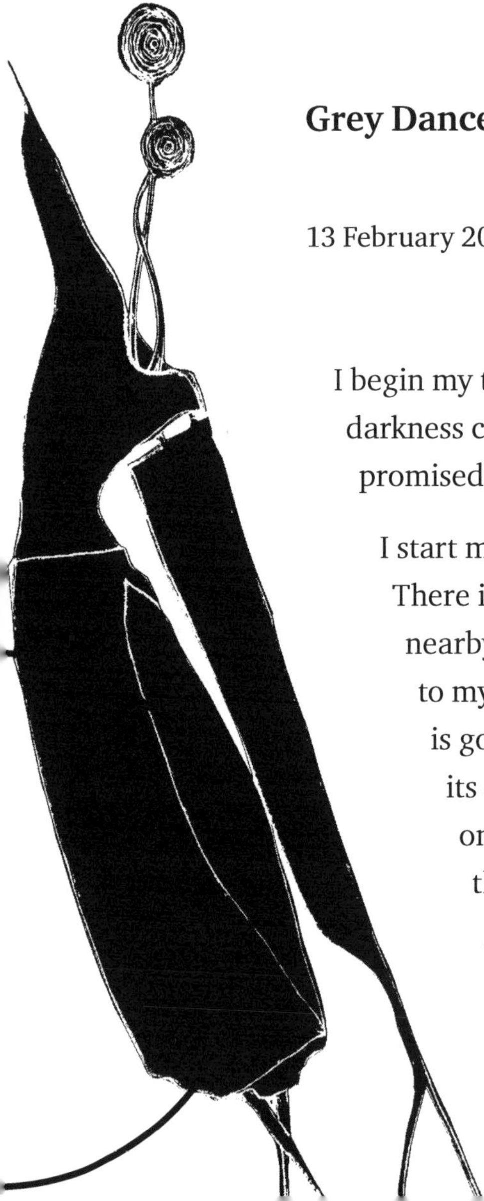

Grey Dance

13 February 2017

I begin my third dance here before complete
darkness comes – contrary to what I had
promised. I just want to move.

I start moving to the singing of the birds.
There is a repeating bird's cry somewhere
nearby, and it gives an impulse
to my movement. Then suddenly that cry
is gone! Somehow, my movement finds
its continuation. Now, it doesn't depend
on the sound. I was set to dance with
the bird's singing, but the singing has
gone! The dance goes beyond my plan
for it, it starts evolving by itself.

I close my eyes because I don't want to see even the scant light that is entering the space. At some point, I am surprised to find the walls and begin dancing with them. In my mind's eye, I see my shaved 'hedgehog' head as grey, just like these coarsely plastered walls that I am connecting with through my head and shoulders, even though my hair probably looks quite blond. This is my exploration of the space and its limits, represented by the two walls.

My dance ended in a very interesting way: a geometrical inclusion of myself into these walls. It felt like I was measuring the space using the length of my arms and the stretching of my spine along one of the walls. There came a pause, a completion. My spine was stretched along the wall, my back pressing against the concrete. My left arm was stretched out completely. I knew that the wall continued beyond my fingertips. My right arm was just long enough to reach the wall that limited my space on the left and bend there, pointing in the direction of the second wall. I was drawn, included, into that corner.

Rocks… Walls… The colour of grey…. It was a grey dance;
quite contained and at the same time slippery, rolling;
it was a quiet, unassuming, cautious dance.

freedomDANCE cycle

14 February

Finally, a dance in the complete darkness has happened.
I had to wait four days for this!

I started on my yoga mat, which became an anchor for me. I have two mats, and I know where I am and how to get to other places if I know where those mats are. So, I started on my mat. I didn't plan to dance. I was doing something else. And then, somehow I felt: here we go – a complete darkness! I was actually enjoying precisely that – when the darkness was absolute.

My eyes are open. There's a circle, a rather narrow circle made up of tree branches or sticks. There are many of them. They are black. They make up a circular fence with somewhat uneven edges. There are lots of feathers hanging, attached to that fence. As I turn around, the whole structure turns with me. Even if I turn my head, the structure turns as well. And now it's gone.

It's fascinating what happens in the darkness.

I am looking at the walls. They are a blend of the darker matter surrounding me at the level of my eyes compared to what is just above and what is just below.

But back to my dance!

A complete darkness!

I start moving from where I am. I don't come to my designated 'dance floor' space. I find an anchor in a circular movement of my head. I am turning, from right to left, over and over again. It is so quiet! I am not isolated from sounds like I am isolated from light. And yet it is a completely quiet moment. There's no music, of course. I can hear something in my neck so clearly – that probably indicates some ailment; there's still something not right there! It's not very nice but it doesn't prevent me from going with a greater range of movement. The head just keeps turning and turning and turning and turning – 360 degrees! And then, I start paying attention to my breath. The breath comes in. It was always there, of course. I am talking about the breath that accentuates the movement, that comes together with the movement, that is an organic part of movement – that kind of breath comes along, and it becomes richer, more interesting. My hands start to move. For a while, I am moving on the same spot. It's a very interesting exploration. Staying on the same little spot in the room. I laugh out loud when I realise that a freedomDANCE cycle is happening!

Here I am starting with the body, engaging the whole body, whatever I can move, on that one spot. And then I can open the space. I move cautiously, but confidently as well.

Yeah, that's how I felt! I knew I was safe, and I was cautious at the same time. I knew that my safe space was limited. As I started moving around, I got more comfortable with it. At some point, my dance acquired a quality of expression: it's not only that I opened the space for myself, I also opened myself to the space. Obviously, I didn't have a partner!

And then, a little Transformation dance came. I shook and melted. I stopped thinking about my body, letting the impulse that came from somewhere other than my mind do something with it – softly, very softly.

I was really fascinated by what happened next and which made it obvious that a freedomDANCE cycle was happening. I slowed down and very cautiously, very slowly, like in a slow-motion film, started exploring the space. And of course, before that, in Transformation, I turned around and moved around quite a bit.

Just to remind you, I was in complete, absolute darkness. Somehow – don't ask how – I knew where the walls were. There are two walls meeting and forming a corner. I thought I was still in that corner. I thought I knew where those walls were. And I started to expand my dance – cautiously – through my hands, through extending my arms, and then making a step. Yes! The wall that I thought was going be there was indeed there! A moment of complete presence came as I started dancing with both walls. I spent some time feeling their support and their tallness compared to my own height.

. . .

It brought back memories and feelings that transcended this dance. I've been 'recapitulating' my life – remembering, trawling through my life again, bringing awareness to those moments when I was going around on autopilot. I didn't expect to have so many memories connected to my father. Something happened in my life that separated me from him. And it took many years for us to come together again. There was no drama or official pronouncements in that separation. And yet for a number of years we were not as closely connected as during my early childhood. I completely forgot about how close I was to him when I was a baby and as a little kid. It's one of the great gifts that I received in the darkness – remembering about our early strong bond and his 100% support as a father.

The support and the tallness of those two walls reminded me of my relationship with my father when I was a little boy. It also dawned on me that I was revising an exercise with a wall that I came up with a few years earlier in Close Friends, an ongoing group in Moscow. I finally got to experience this exercise myself, dancing with the support and the tallness of the wall as a representation of the father.

The ending was fascinating as well. I ended my dance in a frontal contact with the wall. I had my chest, my shoulders, my genitals and thighs, my belly – the whole front of my body touching the wall. I had to lift and throw back my neck, my head so only my chin was touching the wall, leaning into it. I enjoyed staying there; the wall was much cooler than the air. It felt like a perfect ending to a very rich dance. Nothing of this kind had come to me on the dance floor before.

I don't know if I'll continue dancing only in the complete darkness.
It felt special this time.

As I am saying this, I am walking on the same spot because I have lost my orientation! I hope to find my anchors – my yoga mats – so that I can walk back and forth… my nine steps, crossing the room, from one wall to another.

This is my world… for seventeen more days.

…

I just had the idea of creating a video to accompany the words that I've recorded about my dance – Or, to replicate it to some extent. Or, rather to use the motifs from the words that I have recorded and some sound. Something very simple. Mysterious sounds that we can hear from time to time, rather than a melody. I am wearing a *dhoti* wrapped around my hips. And I'm not that visible, really. Grey is the colour. So, I am semi-recognisable. Lights, shapes, outlines, motifs, rather than a realistic portrayal.

Of course, we can't just show darkness. That wouldn't work.

However, there is something that needs to be resolved: I have never been happy enough with my body to show it to others. Somehow, if I'm at the beach or a pool, it's OK. But when it comes to a performance, or a photoshoot, or a dance, I have never been comfortable enough with my body, with the look of it. That needs to change.

I could just dismiss the issue – 'Alex is just thinking about superficial physical beauty.' Or I can head towards a breakthrough and come out of the *kuti* ready for the first time in my life to be photographed or filmed naked or semi-naked, so that my body is fully visible. Yes, I could dismiss it as a nonsense, as something unimportant. Or, I could recognise in this the same deep longing that has been hanging on all the way from my 20s.

When I was a teen, as far as I remember, I was happy with my body. I imagined being visible, showing off. It was more than OK – at least in my imagination. Some time in my 20s, I decided that my body was not something to be shown or photographed. And there has been very little departure from that since then. Just brief moments – Thank you, Todd, who used me as a live model! I wonder if he still has those sketches somewhere – those unusual shapes that my body took naturally and he admired? Not very likely....

It's one of those things that is worth resolving and being able to say later: I had my moment at 46 or 50, whatever. And my body as captured on camera is good to see.

. . .

I had an interesting experience on the floor when I lay down on my mat after the dance. Suddenly, my arms started dancing and it seemed to me that they were grey shadows that moved, and that I saw my arms and how they interacted with each other. In other words, I saw the dance of my arms in some kind of unclear grey definition as if I saw their shadows. *And* I know that that's not possible. Perhaps my mind can imagine so well what is moving, where exactly and how, that it can work it out based on my kinesthetic sense without my eyes. And yet, I had a clear sensation of seeing even though it wasn't possible. I can't see anything else here! If I move one of my hands right next to my eyes I don't see any difference. It's fascinating how one can see what one doesn't see. The mind can see instead of the eyes.

Surfaces

15 February 2017

Today I moved.

All those discussions about what is dance and what is movement! Well, I think that today I moved.

I don't think it was a dance. In a way, it was… and yet I prefer to say that I moved.

I was naked. It was dark.

I wasn't as good at finding my orientation in the space as on other days. I was going somewhere thinking there would be a wall and I got to my bed instead! I had to search for the walls and stay with them. It was a pleasant sensation to be with the walls because they are so cool – so smooth and so cool. It's incredibly hot in here. I think it's the second hottest day I've had so far.

I just moved.

Or I danced?

If it was a dance, it was a dance of surfaces: The surfaces of the walls and the surfaces of my body.

I was slowly finding my way in the corner: touching the walls with all the surfaces that I've got.

Then, at some point, I started smelling myself.

There was a vivid component of smell. This room is surrounded by three sets of walls. The windows are located at different levels and covered with extremely thick mosquito nets. The air doesn't really travel that easily, if at all.

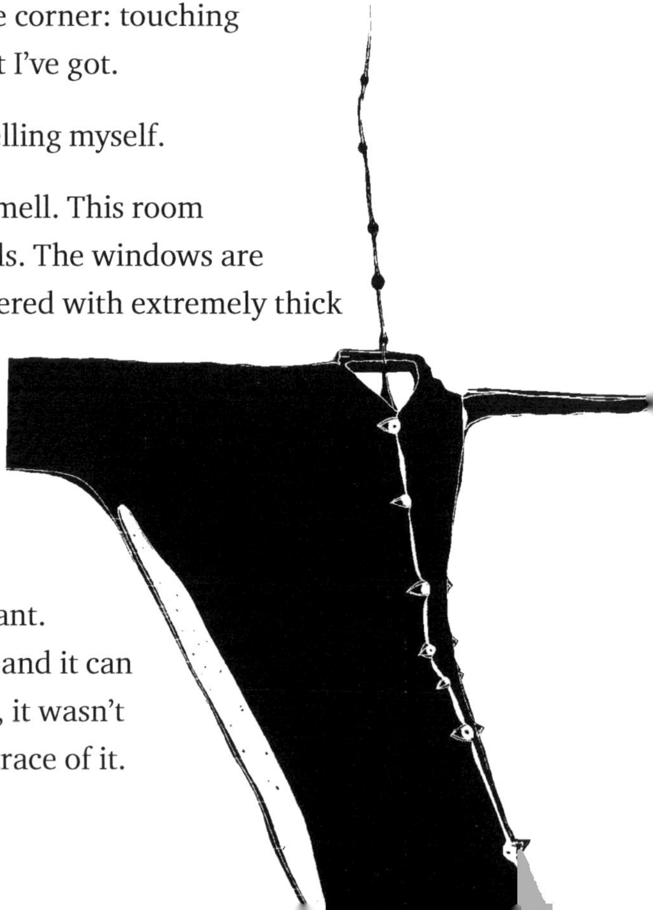

One morning, I detected a familiar smell of a tree that grows here at Athreya. This smell is normally quite strong but pleasant. Well, it smells a little bit like soap and it can be too much. But here, in the *kuti*, it wasn't strong at all. I could detect just a trace of it.

On another occasion, I smelled something else – only in one part of the room, the one which is on the same side as the entrance. The entrance to the *kuti* faces a barn – there are three cows and a little calf that spend their nights there, and they get their food there as well. All of sudden, I smelt a tiny hint of manure – just a trace, not like a real smell, but enough to recognise it. And that was nice.

Otherwise, I can't smell anything really, except myself. I smell more here than I usually do. It's interesting to notice the difference in the smell of my forearms and my elbows, where the arm bends at the elbow, and shoulders, and armpits. It's not a bad smell but I do smell! Most of the time I am not aware of it.

Here's another and maybe shocking detail about my stay here. The classical version of this meditation calls for no shower for however long you stay in the kuti. I am allowed to bathe but I am not encouraged to. So, I'll see how long I can go without. So far, four days with no shower. And there's more of my smell on me. The dance of smell and surfaces.

Here is another thing that happens here. Although it's dark, it doesn't seem to be dark. When I finally get to that wall that I missed the first time around I think it is covered with mosaic depicting some kind of a wave pattern. I can see the colours. Everything is blinking. I see fish, and other shapes. I imagine them being here on the wall. I imagine them just being in the space, hanging in the air like a hologram.

I always see something here. It surprises me. I never thought that I was a visual person. But here… I begin to walk and all of a sudden yellow geographical shapes appear in front of me. Or, now it may be human silhouettes. They are beautiful, too – as if a talented artist designed them! It's all there, it's all in my mind somehow, it's within reach.

Right now, I come to standing and there's no way I can call what I see darkness. I am thinking of teaching a retreat called 'Meeting Emptiness' as a follow-up to this experience. Maybe I need to find a better name for it! It doesn't look like emptiness at all. It is full of all sorts of shapes. Now, for example, there are outer space ship shapes out there!

My vision is uneven here, too, as if the lighting is uneven. I mostly see with my right eye, and my left eye seems to be blind – just darkness there.

There are all sorts of things going on visually. I see a lot of red – all different shades. This morning, I was doing push-ups. And I experienced the exercise in colour – as a definite, in your face, red.

Now it seems like someone has put the lights on. It's not just red… it's alive as if there was a real live fire in the space. This is really cool – as if someone is lighting a fire right under my feet! But I know that there's nothing there! It's really incredible.

. . .

Everything seems to have settled now somehow.

God, I love the darkness. I wonder if I could be in total darkness all the time somehow. That would be so much fun!

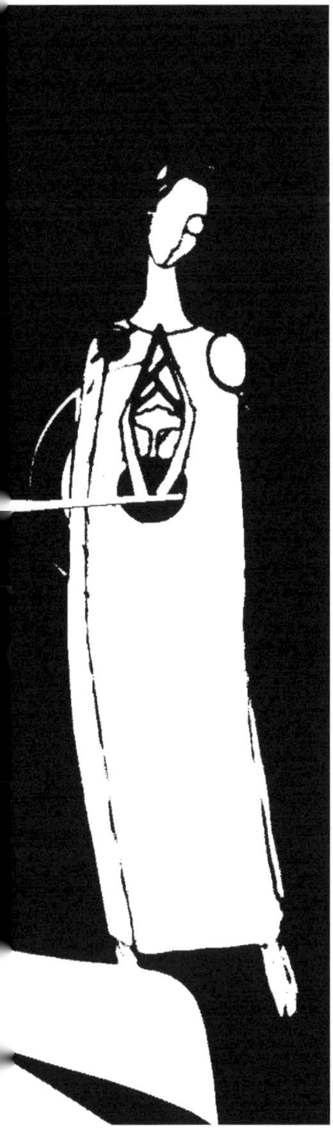

Sculptures

16 February 2017

I danced naked again. Today, I think, was the hottest day so far. It's not so much the darkness but the heat that makes it challenging being here…

Today I don't have the same extravaganza of visual effects as before. Still, it seems that there's always something in front of me – as if I'm going to walk into something. But it's more or less dark overall…

And still I'm not dancing in an empty space. First, I see some vegetation. Then there are antique sculptures and I start imagining what kind of shape I would take if I were to become an antique sculpture. And, of course, my mind interferes: Shall I cover my genitals or shall I leave them visible? That is my way into my dance.

This way, I am discovering and opening my body. Then I move towards the wall and roll slowly, turning my head and shoulders along one wall, then another. I move as if I am measuring the walls. How many turns are there? How far can I extend my arm and still be touching the wall? I think for a moment: Maybe the dance is not happening tonight? Maybe I'll just hang out here for a while. (Thinking back, I didn't realise that I was opening the space that way!)

Then I move into the centre of my little square where I can dance without any interference, still being careful because there's a bed, two walls and a yoga mat limiting the space. I have a little dance in the middle and then come back to the walls.

. . .

To be honest, I forgot what followed… The more I got into movement, the more it felt like a dance – an experience.

There was an ending – of course there was.

Oh, that's a shame that I forgot almost everything! I only remember that I came back to the sculptures thread at the end. I ended in a particular posture. I could have been a sculpture – and that time, unlike in the beginning, I wasn't worried whether my genitals were exposed or not.

That was my dance tonight. In total darkness. Completely naked.

It was also very quiet. An almost complete silence – which does not happen here often. The *kuti* is in the middle of a busy Ayurvedic clinic. There are people walking, there are animals that produce the milk that I am given – they are right there at the entrance – there are birds. I can hear those things. But, for some reason, at the moment when I decided to dance, it was so quiet. The silence added something to the experience. It was really empty on many levels. Only the one thing was there – something that filled that emptiness completely – *the heat*!

In the Rays of Black

17 February 2017

It was the longest dance today so far. One reason for this was that the dance didn't come readily. It wasn't forthcoming. I felt really sleepy and disoriented. It took me a long time to arrive into something that really felt like a dance. I was moving and exploring. There were interesting moments. I thought: Oh, this is it! This is really cool! The dance is kicking in! But the doors that were opening led nowhere. There was a moment… and then the moment was gone.

I found a different kind of a corner for the first time; not the inside of the corner, but the outer edge of the corner. It's a quite sharp edge where two walls meet. It felt like that ridge dissected me right through the middle, through my buttocks (two buttocks – left and right), along the spine (left and right), middle of the head, two legs and two arms. And I thought: Oh this is cool! I want to stay with this! But then, it was too painful, too sharp, and I moved on.

My head pressed against the wall. (My hair is quite short and that is very unfamiliar. I haven't had my hair this short since I was a little kid.) The sound and the sensation and the toughness of the wall's grip – that kind of contact was very unfamiliar. I thought: This must be it! I've found my anchor! It's not even my head, it's my hair that's going to hold my dance together! But in a moment, it was gone. The interest was gone!

I kept going from one place to another. I almost gave up hope of dancing! I tried to get on my toes and stretch upwards but I didn't manage to do it; it's much harder to do in the dark than with the lights on! I tried it again. It didn't quite work. I tried it again. Oh, yeah, this time it worked!

That was the start of what I can call a dance. I didn't really think about it when I was dancing. An idea, quick as lightning in the sky, crossed my mind: this is the dance! This is what I call the dance! It's not all that preparation or organising myself. It's when something effortless emerges, or one thing just leads into the next without a choreography or a disjunction or any time to think

is it this or that, is it a beginning or is it the ending, or is it a pause? All of these things can happen but they don't need to have a name. They don't need to be designated. They don't need to be recognised as such. Because everything is one. And that's why I love dancing. Because I think that's my aspiration for my life: everything is one. Full stop.

So, this oneness happened. And that's definitely not a dance that I ever had before – I wish I had…

I was naked. I sensed my skin and I touched my stomach. 'Oh, my God! I am the skinniest that I've been for years! ' I didn't just lose my belly, I got skinnier than… I don't know… than I have been for many years, let's put it that way. In my imagination, I had this shiny sparkly black tightly fitted outfit on, covering my body or most of it. My body was elongated. There were pauses and weird twists of my hips and my spine, and limbs and head as I moved. My dance was very crooked and complex and unpredictable and at the same time there was a fluidity to it, somehow, and a beauty. I was moving and it seemed that my movement, the movement of my naked body in the dance, was somehow projected onto the screen where I saw myself doing those movements wearing the shiny black, maybe leather, outfit. And that felt good!

And then it was over. I found myself not where I thought I was in the space. I started exploring that spot. And there was richness to this part of my dance as well. I explored the levels truly for the first time since I've been here. I have been very reluctant to get on the floor in here, for some reason. It's quite cold and maybe not clean enough and I can't see. So I just don't go on the floor. And then today, I did.

Tonight's dance wasn't only the longest, it was also the most expansive dance so far. I used more space than I have before in these last six days – both horizontally – I think I used two thirds of the space – and also vertically. I finally got down on the floor – that was fun.

And, as usual, there was something else interesting which I forgot… like one forgets a dream. You know that it was interesting and meaningful, but you can't remember however hard you try.

. . .

I think what I have just described would be a cool video – That shiny black, tightly fitted outfit and the quirky movements. Maybe set to music and maybe with some text and maybe with a short rendition of this account.

Every movement exploration in the darkness so far has been fascinating. It's been unlike anything I do normally.

When I first started moving I thought I would keep my eyes open, but it doesn't make much difference really. Sometimes it does but most of the time, in this darkness, it's the same picture whether I open my eyes or close them. The dance happened when I did close my eyes. I gave up, I kind of lost the discipline, I forgot about it, and somehow that triggered a shift. So I did that dance of tonight with my eyes closed.

When I started moving, the darkness had a texture or a geometry for me. I'll try to describe what I saw, what I thought the landscape was. Imagine a grey space. Everything is grey. And then imagine a stage or some sort of raised platform. And it's all grey. Not black – grey. Now, imagine some

light projectors, some lights. There are projected lights that expand from their respective sources and intersect. This kind of lighting design is used all the time now: a number of different beams of light intersecting with each other. The next step may require a real leap of imagination! Try to picture that instead of light these devices are projecting blackness into the grey space. That was my landscape. I thought: Wow, this is really cool! I am going to dance in the multiple spotlights of blackness, intersecting, moving pillars of total darkness. Grey is quite dark, but not completely so.

. . .

Oh, God, I love to dance so much!

My hip feels much better – touch wood. I can do weird stuff with my hips. A couple of times tonight I was like: oh-oh, it's probably gonna hurt! But then it was all fine. It feels great to be able to move freely and graciously and quirkily and slowly as well. *Yeah.* A good dance and a good aftertaste.

. . .

Dance helps me develop some appetite. I am not supposed to take medicines if I can't fully digest them. I need to be hungry every time before taking the medicines. And I am getting hungry! From tonight on, I'll be taking medicated oil in addition to my sweet disgusting jam, which stopped being disgusting to me. I just don't even want to imagine what kind of oil it's going to be. Well, it's the only nutrition I get. Day six. Tomorrow this time it will be my first full week here.

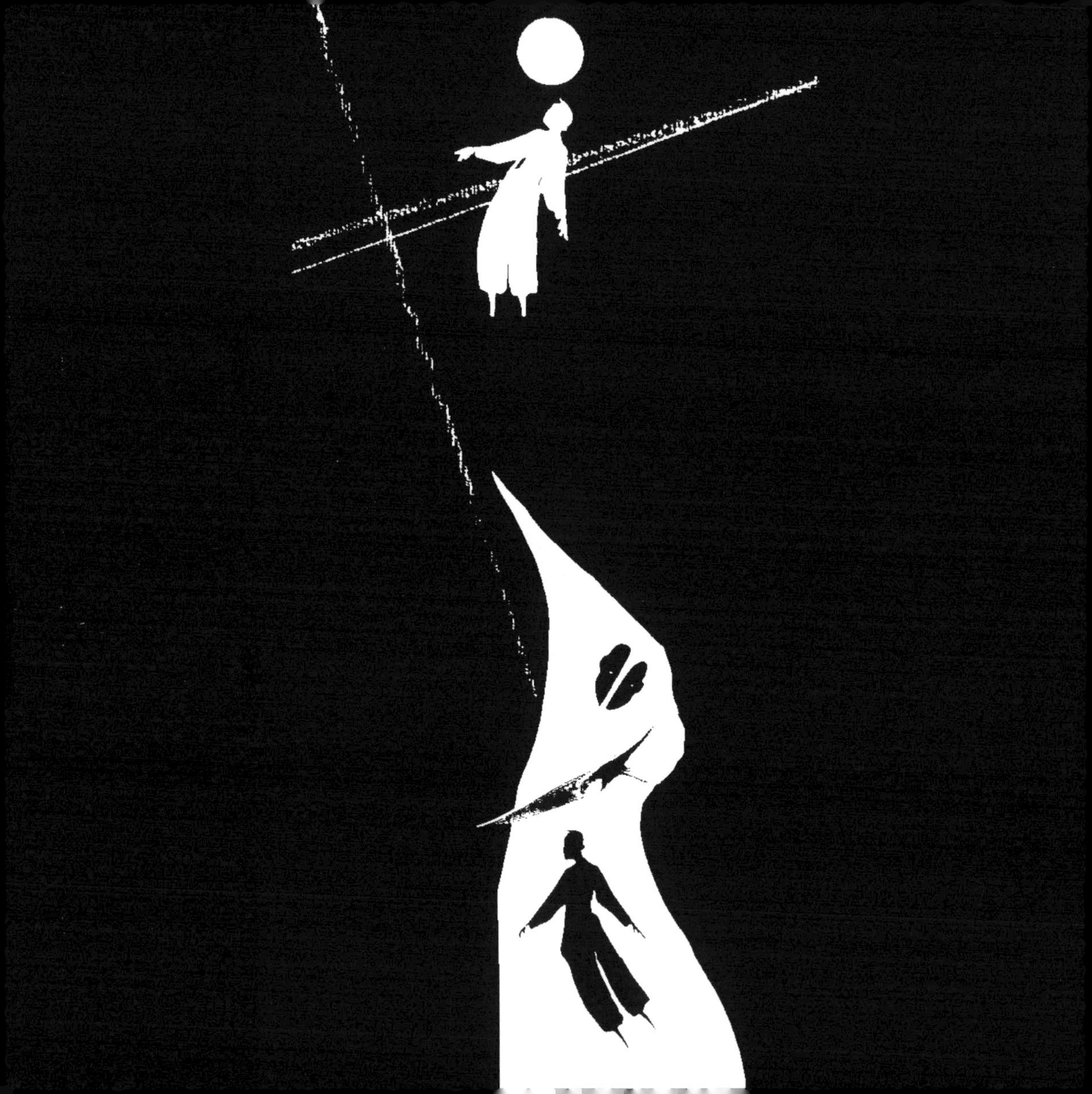

Drums and Waiting

19 February 2017

I am struggling to think what to say about tonight's dance.
So, I'd better just say it.

So there were drums again. And I joined in.

I had a *déjà vu* moment. That has happened to me before, albeit not in the same rare setting for a dance class. Maybe it has happened to you as well. Sometimes, you walk into a dance space and you think: "This sound system sucks. What is this crappy sound about?" It felt a little bit like that for me because I could hear the drums but could not quite hear them. Sometimes, they were fully audible, and sometimes extremely faint… Maybe the drums did get louder outside, with the evening approaching, with the darkness arriving, or maybe I tuned in better. Whatever the case, maybe after a while I thought: "Wow! That's a really good sound system! Why did I complain before? I can dance to it, no problem whatsoever!"

So the drums where there for me. And they were really good drums. There was a musician from Jordan called Ramsey here. He tried to find out where the sound of the drums comes from but no-one seems to know! It's another one of my dreams now for my life after the *kuti* – to find out! I'll come out on a Saturday evening. (At least that's what I am planning.) I will wonder around and ask and find these hidden drummers. Maybe they have a recording? Or maybe I can just take someone's number, get their names? It seems to be a regular Saturday practice. I'm not sure whether there is dancing to it. They play quite fast. They are not novices. It's not like they are rehearsing the same piece, again and again. They just go on with a minimum of interruption between the compositions.

There's just a little bit of a pause. I am imagining that they just pause to take a breath. And then, they go to the next one.

What shall I call my experience tonight? A semi-disco! Don't know how to describe it. I danced a lot. They played almost without interruption. And I took breaks. At some point, I remember, I took a break and lay on my stomach and did an exercise for my hip that Eva, another patient here and a physiotherapist, taught me. Then I joined in dancing again. Then I went to the toilet. On another occasion, I took a drink. There were interruptions. That's not how our practice goes normally. I am used to dancing, dancing non-stop, but that's not what I did tonight.

My dancing was mostly about waiting. I've learned to wait in my dance. Waiting is what brought me to dance meditation in the first place. I will never forget how I went clubbing in Brighton. I'd had a chronic neck pain for many years then. My neck was particularly stiff that night. I didn't enjoy being on the dance floor; I could not move freely. And then, after a couple of hours of staying with what I can't even call a dance today, staying with that bounce on one spot, waiting for something else to happen, – boom! wow! Something actually happened! My neck released, my shoulders went down letting my head to move. I had a beautiful dance – enjoyable, free!

So, I was waiting for moments of freedom tonight. My hip hurt. It hurts in a new way now, but it hurts. There's something going on. Something is shifting and changing in my hip. I couldn't just go for it. I was even trying to shake using one leg for support. It turns out that even if I am putting all my weight on my left leg, somehow my right hip still gets engaged, still gets affected and hurts. I was waiting and experimenting. Shaking works to some extent. What I have to avoid is unpredictable movement of my hips – but that's what I love! And it doesn't work for me any more. As long as it is a patterned, predictable movement that does not hurt, I think I can go quite a long way. That's possible with shaking – releasing the head and hands. So, I did a lot of that. I feel that it's really good for me. Because in everything else I do, even the dancing that I do, there's no shaking and release of that sort – for the neck or for the hands. I found it quite therapeutic and helpful. It wasn't the best dance of my life in terms of its depth and ease, but I kept going for a long time. I didn't want to stop, obviously. I could stop at any moment! I dropped out, and then I came back. I started experimenting with more continuous movements to the drums. And that worked. At some point, I did do quite a lot with my hips and the pain went away and then it came back. I am not talking about huge pain but I want to be really sensitive and not push or exaggerate. I want to heal rather than harm myself. When the pain was gone, there was a feeling of freedom in my hips. Maybe for 15 seconds I had my moment of joy and remembered how my dance used to be – that it was all about hips, all about the juice that's in the hips.

What am I going to do? This is the method! This is the method! It's the core, the centre that needs to be engaged! I am finding a new way, finding a new centre I guess.

I experimented for quite a long time. Obviously, the drummers did not come to drum for merely 5 minutes. They drummed maybe for an hour, maybe an hour and a half.

As I was recording this, I kept my eyes closed – visualising, reliving my dance, and so I missed the moment when the last bits of light disappeared from the space. So, it is evening now. Time to prepare for dinner (well, medicines and a delicious glass of warm milk!) and then say my prayers. And then brush my teeth. And then sleep. Just a normal evening in my darkroom.

Birds

20 February 2017

I just had another dance
in darkness, complete darkness.

The whole day I've been
struggling a bit. I've been
struggling with hip pain.
It got better, I think… Sort
of better – by the evening.

And still, I doubted
I could dance.

For some reason, I'd made
this decision coming in that
I would dance every day.
So, OK, let's dance…

There were some drums again. But they were in the distance and they quickly disappeared. All I could hear was the birds – their cries. There were not that many. They were just there now and again. I started moving with these sounds. And then everything became silent. There was not a sound. I continued to move.

It was a very bendy dance. I was bending to the sides. I was bending backwards. Not so much forwards, for some reason. Backwards. I am in an excellent shape actually. I remember about 10 years ago, I indulged in bending backwards and touching the floor with my hands behind my back. I can do that now… well, almost!

There was no music, and no one and nothing rushed me.

It was very simple. Well, the movement wasn't simple – just easy. I was cruising pleasure. The pleasure of movement, the pleasure of feeling my body, the pleasure of feeling the touch, the air, the body parts touching, the body touching the walls.

All of a sudden, the birds started crying again. One bird was going, 'O-O-O-O-O-O' – a pattern. But then many of them did it at the same time. When multiple birds do a patterned cry but without coordinating with each other that breaks the pattern, that's Transformation! I could not stop myself. I forgot about the hip and just danced to it. I was moved by those sounds.

Then it all settled and only one bird at a time would repeat the pattern, now and then. It offered a very different invitation. It had a very different effect on my body, and my dance changed.

And then I just got tired. I get tired so quickly when the complete darkness comes. I found a wall. Both of my hands were pushing the wall. And the birds were still going on. I thought they needed to stop, but they wouldn't. So there was this soundtrack of the crazy last cries before it got completely dark outside and me doing a very geometrical repetitive exploration to it. That exploration included me giving my weight to the wall, and stretching my back and opening my buttocks and pressing my feet to the floor – all sort of different things. I repeated every movement that I discovered a few times. There was the chaotic music created by the birds and me doing very structured dance. I was playing time after time repeating the same movements. Those movements were very imaginative; I've never done anything like that.

Then it turned into something sweet… a sweet surrender of giving my weight to the wall. Using all sorts of surfaces of my body as a point where I could have contact. It was a moment of very soft touch. Slowing. Settling. Calming down. Getting quiet. Only now I couldn't wait for the birds to stop their noise. They did settle – just not all of them! Only now as I am speaking into the dictaphone, are they finally settling.

Tonight's dance started out not so promising and turned into a beautiful experience. The beautiful experience that reassured me. I am so happy! I am in such good shape. I am in such good shape as a mover… Oh, forget about one leg! Even with one hip being difficult most of the time I can do a lot.

In the middle of that dance, all of sudden, I had a flash of fear: What will my students say now? What will they say? I used to be very militant about my advice: Dance only with those teachers who dance themselves! We need to practise what we preach. Trust those teachers of this practice who actually practice. Well, I am making a commitment to myself: even with a painful hip, I am going to dance once a week. I am not going to dance more. I will protect my hip by limiting my time on the dance floor. I will find a dance that I can do and I will savour it. I hope that I can even discover the dance that can do me, even with this hip being, at least at the moment, not in the best shape. I am going to savour that one class that I afford to give myself in a given week. I'll be OK. I will still be a practising teacher.

Singing

21 February 2017

I think I can have a tick for
the dance of the day.

It just happened spontaneously.
I was waiting for my ‘food’
at lunch time and all of a sudden,
I caught myself singing.

I started dancing to it. It was
playful and provocative. I even
touched my nipples and they
were hard. And I did a few other
things… And then it stopped.
I don’t know if I will dance
again in the evening. But I’ve
done my dance of the day!

And what about singing? Oh, my God, I was indeed singing! Now, I know that it takes me 10 days of isolation to have a spontaneous urge to sing. Interesting! I thought it would be earlier than that!

My busy life here includes chanting. Maybe that counts as singing, just a different kind?

What else have I been doing?

I've been praying.

I've been doing yoga.

I've been recording myself recapitulating my life.

If you think of it, there's been a lot of voice! The first three or four days, I was struggling with that. I thought I was using my voice too much. Now it's much better. Although I think sometimes that I am losing my voice a little bit. Well, despite being in isolation I am talking almost nonstop. Who would've thought it!

Hips

24 February 2017

Tonight's dance felt more like
a movement exploration.

That's an on-going debate:
What is it, the dance? How
is it different from movement?

Well, in my humble opinion,
what happened tonight
was closer to movement.

I am really weak. I can mobilise
myself for a short time.
But overall, I want to stay
lying down on the floor.

Still, I got up thinking that maybe a dance would come. I had a *dhoti*, the traditional dress, on. It was wrapped all around my hips. I started moving my hips and being extremely careful with them. I've been tracking the pain, and the tension, and the inflammation. For a few days, they have been better than before. I know 'the problem' is still there. It's not gone. In my dreams, yes, I am thinking: I've healed myself! But I know that if I move without taking care there will be pain.

So, I wanted to see what I could actually do with my hips without inviting pain. It turned out that I could do a lot! It was somewhat controlled, somewhat premeditated. But then there were moments when I just moved my hips any way they wanted to move and there was only one instance when it hurt.

Soon I needed support. With difficulty, I found the walls. I was happy to be supported. I went on my knees, crossed my ankles and crossed my hands. That was an unusual position to be in. And that's where my movement found completion and became stillness.

A Wake-Up Dance

27 February 2017

OK, tonight I danced to one tune, again
and again. It was my internal music,
a simple melody that came to me.

I've been missing music! I am so ready
to dance to a good, long, clubby track.
And that's what I created in my head.

I actually started moving first.
Then the music came and
I stayed with it. There were
birds crying. And there were
voices outside. And there
was my simple melody
playing inside my head,
again and again.

I stayed with it for a while. My movement was probably not so imaginative but it was more active than before. It felt like dancing in a disco. Some release came in my dance, with fluidity in my spine and my head. And then it all stopped.

Yet my dance really woke me up. I slept today in the day time. I woke up shortly before it started getting completely dark. I was still very sleepy. It's very hot and humid in here, and I was thinking:

What am I going to do?

I need to lie on the floor.

I have no energy.

There's no air.

And then I started moving. And now I feel awake. My problems didn't go away: It is still hot, there's still not much air. And yet, I am moving, walking back and forth, drinking water, getting ready to pray. It will be a prayer for the dead. I'll start with my mother. Today is her birthday. I am glad I've danced on her birthday. I am dedicating this day of my life to her. I will spend the rest of it in prayer.

Flopping onto the Floor

28 February 2017

Today I danced before lunch. I was already getting quite weak and sleepy by then.

My dance had two parts to it.

The first part I was having a floppy dance. I assumed that it would grow, it would somehow get the energy going. I used a little bit of space, but in the end stayed on one spot. My body was moving on the same spot in a floppy way.

The growth, the explosion never happened. The floppiness took me down. I ended up with my head and my hands on the floor and my bum sticking out. I stayed there for a while. I thought: that was it. And then I felt a pull to go down completely.

Oh, my glorious mind! Once again, I thought: the floor is not very clean for my naked body to be rolling around. I actually interrupted what was happening to put my shorts and a t-shirt on! Then, I came down on the floor. I enjoyed a nice stretch followed by turning and twisting on the floor. I realised how much I missed it – a nice floor and a soft track at the beginning of a class – a space for arriving into my dance. In this case, it WAS the dance. There was nothing that came out of that, except a posture. At some point, I was done.

I miss being on the dance floor, in a class, and stretching on the floor so much! Using the floor as support, as an ally… as a bed. I'll get there!

My day-time dance inspired me to take one of my *dhotis* and spread the cloth on the floor where I have my dance space. I am lying on it on the floor and waiting; who knows, maybe I will do a little bit more movement… if it comes…

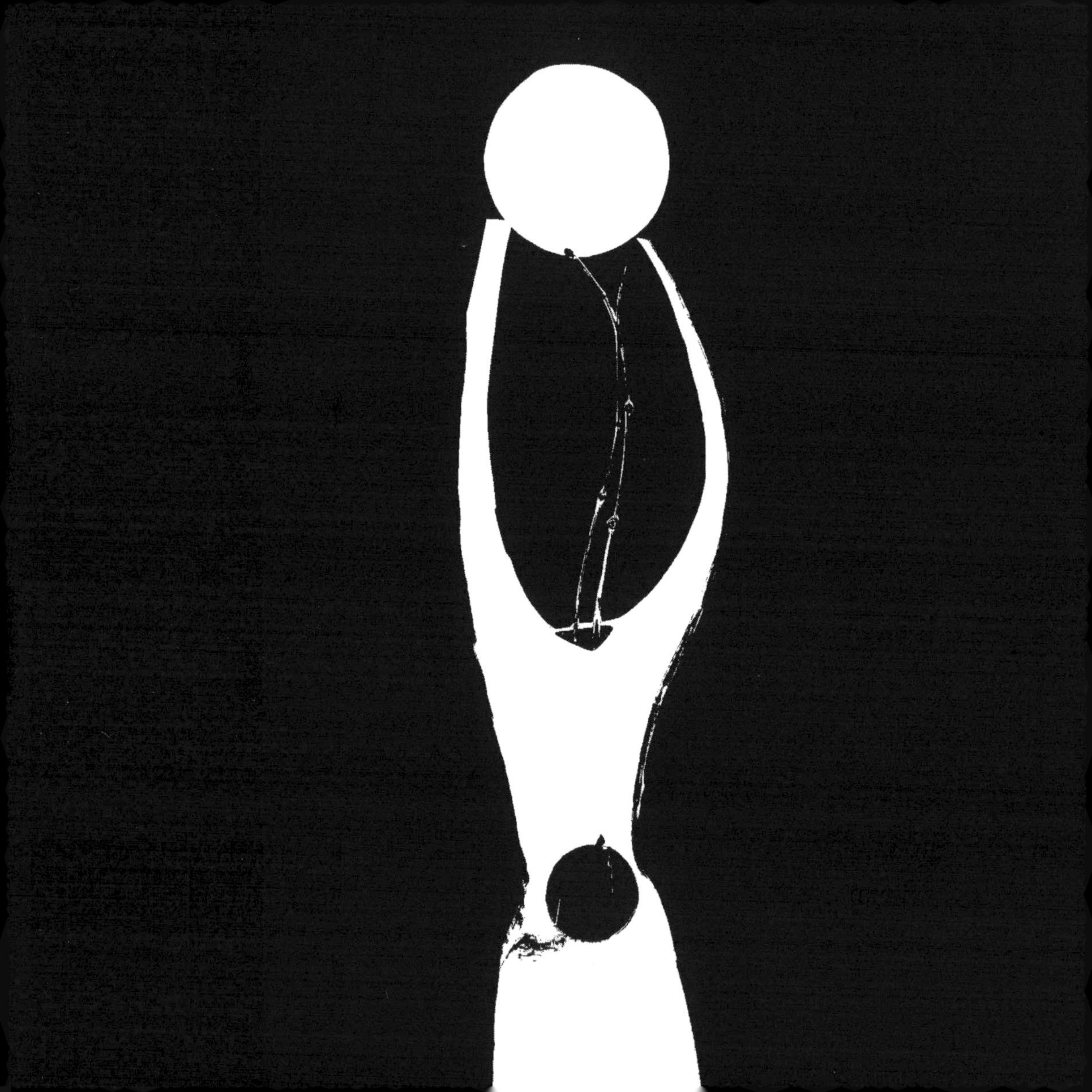

Head as a Gateway into Dance

1 March 2017

Finally, I danced in the morning! Right after my yoga, meditation and fitness exercises. I put my underwear on and started moving. And again, I noticed this – quite often it's the head that takes me into my dance, it's the head that's the doorway into movement. The head was moving quite gently and in a circular way and then the whole body joined – the arms and the chest and the spine. A wavy type of movement. It was really pleasant and soft and light. Tender as well.

All of a sudden the movement started growing. A freedomDANCE cycle happened. Do I need to use freedomDANCE language all the time? A dance cycle happened! I was so happy – simple as that!

Sway with Me

3 March 2017

I just had a dance that was promising to be a forced dance. It was the only time that I could dance; I'd forgotten to do it earlier! I felt awful – sleepy and just awful. I am really sleepy now, too.

Lying on the floor was the only thing I could do, it seemed. Yet I did get up. My head was pressing against the wall but I didn't want to do that! And then, I got into the middle of my dance space, and a sway came – from side to side, from side to side… swaying. The whole body started following, building momentum, while my arms were hanging listlessly. I got into the sway and I actually heard a familiar song inside my head – that 'sway with me' track. Little by little, I became more alive, I was at least moving. And then from the hips some turns came and some steps as well. Oh, yeah, I was moving! That was great!

Then, the tiredness took over again, I slowed down and that was it. I went on the floor to rest. Now, that wasn't a kind of dance that would make you go: 'Wow! What a great dance! ' But it was a dance! It was my dance of today.

. . .

I am 24 hours away from coming out of here. And it is proving to be more difficult to stay here until the end, to stay here as long as I'd decided I would stay, than I ever imagined. I don't know what that says about me.

I am trying to use freedomDANCE structure in order to explain it:
Beginning – middle – end, or, Opening – Transformation – Freedom.

Beginning was great. I was really enthusiastic.
Everything was going very easily.

Transformation: a great physical challenge. That heat! And trying not to sleep during the day. Physically, it was like torture to stay awake when the whole body was asking: 'OK, let me just sleep.'

And now, Freedom: Allowing myself to sleep and getting my sleep patterns completely messed up. And again, I'm suffering physically. Back to square one. *And* an overactive mind, *and* finding excuses:

Maybe I shouldn't stay here till the end?
Maybe it's not good for me?
Maybe it doesn't make sense to spend extra time here?
Let's come out tomorrow morning!
Or, what about I come out now?

Let's renegotiate!
I don't have to do this!

And there's another part of my mind that is saying: You actually changed your whole trip, got new visas to Sri Lanka and India just so that you could stay *longer* in here. So, just stay for three weeks *for God's sake*!

And, yeah, I am staying. But somehow I am feeling like tomorrow may be even more difficult. What is supposed to be Freedom, at the moment at least, does not feel like freedom at all! It feels like a confinement, imprisonment.

I don't know yet what to make out of it.

Going faster than I should again?

Trying to get somewhere before it's time?

Wanting to be over with something that is not complete yet?

Ready to leave, possibly, some gifts behind without discovering them?

Not willing to go to some of those dark rooms, not turning the lights on, not discovering the gifts that are waiting for me when I actually can?

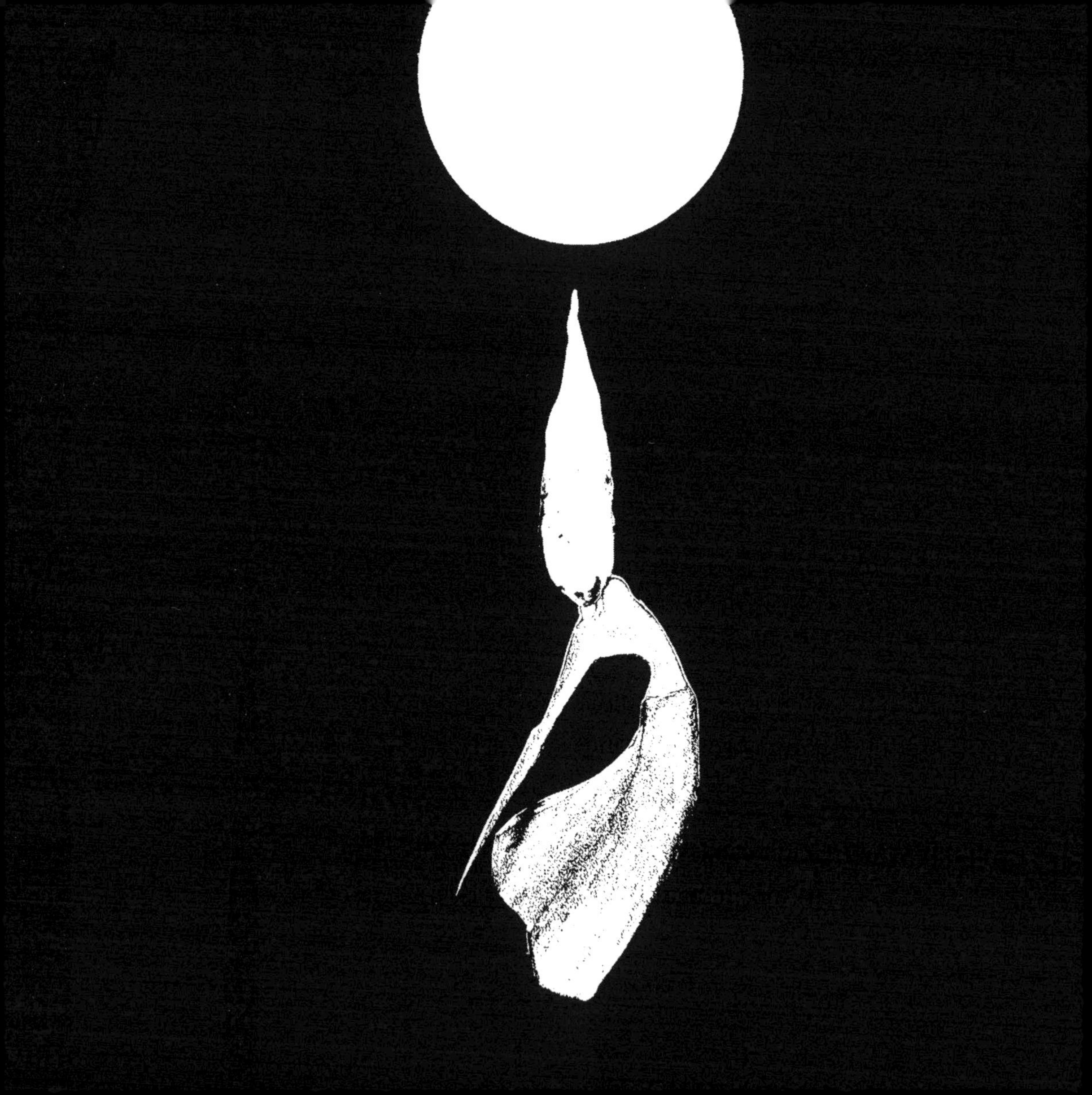

Thank You, *Kuti*

An Afterword

Just to confirm, I did stay in the *kuti* for three weeks – exactly as planned. During the last day of my stay in the *kuti* I was allowed (and encouraged!) to spend some time in the outermost layer of the structure where I could look at the world outside from the windows. I remember spending a lot of time looking at a cow who was left to stay next to the building that day, for some reason. I was watching her, every move she made and that distracted me from counting minutes. I must have picked up something gathering in the air and felt very tired, went to my room and dozed off on my bed. A rain came on that day, which is very unusual for that season in Kerala. Instead of 'packing' as I was planning, I spent the last couple of hours sleeping to the sounds of the rain on the roof and enjoying the cooler air that came with the rain. Someone actually had to wake me up: "It's time to come out! You're not planning to stay here longer, are you?"

I couldn't have wished for a better evening to come out. A real bonus! Everything was so clean and fresh after the rain. And there were still a few drops to fall on my skin here and there. Yes, yes, that skin that had not been touched by water for three weeks! My sense of smell was sharp as never before. I could pick up how each plant had a different scent, as if every tree, bush and flower were speaking to me in the language that only they knew.

. . .

I had a perfect plan for coming out of the *kuti* and I was going to stick with it! I headed straight to the swing that the clinic had. It was some distance from my cabin. Maybe I was a circus performer in one of my previous lives or maybe I have to become one in the next incarnations because, one way or the other, the swing is my single most favourite made-made object on earth. My plan was to get on that swing and watch the sunset while travelling through the air.

. . .

There was a beautiful sunset… but the swing was broken! Do you think I was disappointed? Not in the slightest! I was amazed to notice my natural acceptance of whatever life was offering me and my willingness to let go of my own dreams. Something had definitely shifted!

A recent conversation with one of the dancers has helped me realise how the freedomDANCE cycle really relates to my experience in the *kuti*. The 'happy phase' that came first was the Opening. During those few days, I was given resources to sustain the process. Most importantly, I re-connected with the fundamental condition of love. That really helped me to go through the Transformation phase that lasted for rest of my stay – with all its challenges and struggles. It was only when I came out that I entered into Freedom! Doesn't it make a perfect sense?!

. . .

In case you are curious, I am still dancing and I am still teaching. I am limiting my workshop time away from home to eleven weekends per year – complying with what came to me in the *kuti*. I have created a workshop called From Fear to Love that directly stems from my emotional experience in the *kuti*. I have restructured and enriched our teacher training programmes and made many other changes in my teaching as a result of this experience. And there are so many ideas that I still have to implement! Most importantly, I came out with a sense of joy for having freedomDANCE. I am now proud of having started this school as opposed to being quiet or even almost embarrassed about it earlier.

Of course, there's much more to my *kuti* experience than just what I've gained as a dancer and teacher. People often ask me whether I am going to do it again. I don't know. Maybe in a few years. Not any sooner than that. There are so many lessons that I need to process and integrate into my life! And this will take years. Spending three weeks in the darkness was great. Not for its own sake, however, but because this experience has a lasting potential to change for the better the way I am in my everyday life – more content, accepting, forgiving and loving.

. . .

I went back to the *kuti* at the dawn of the next day. I had to make sure I had collected all my belongings – who would've thought that I wouldn't manage to prepare and would have to leave in a rush! It was good that I went back there. I found myself pulled onto the floor in the middle of the room. I felt my tears rolling down my face. I started to speak and I was speaking for a long time. I did remember to press the 'Rec' button on the dictaphone. It turned out later that it ran out of power at some point. I am still happy I know some of the words that I said and I can share at least them:

Good morning, kuti.

I am here to say goodbye and to release
you, to vacate you, to make you
available for someone else.

May you serve them as well as you served me.
May you hold them as safely as you held me.
May you challenge them as lovingly
as you challenged me.

Thank you, kuti, for sheltering me, for
screening everything that could interfere,
that would want to come from outside.
I know now that I have enough.

Thank you, kuti, for the tears that I cried
here. They brought cleansing, release.

Thank you, kuti, for the memories of the moments of bliss in my life, so different and so many. I am blissed and blessed.

Thank you, kuti, for showing me so clearly that the base line, the fundamental human condition is love. That's what feeds me, that's what can carry me on. Yeah, I was living in love here.

Thank you, kuti, for making me realise that I am a good person. I have good intentions. I work hard. I love. I forgive. I want to do my best! And often I do my best.

Thank you, kuti, for having the space for me to dance every day.

Thank you, kuti, for the melodies that sometimes came into my mind and helped me dance.

The Author

Alex Svoboda, Ph.D., is the founder of freedomDANCE, a school of dance meditation and conscious movement. The liberating power of dance seems to flow naturally out of him and spread to those who dance with him. Alex has lived in three countries, studied at five universities and colleges and worked as an analyst, manager and training facilitator at the world's leading organisations, including the legendary consultancy McKinsey & Company and London Business School. He is a published author of academic articles and a book. He lives in London and teaches internationally. Additional information about Alex and freedomDANCE is available at www.freedom-dance.com.

The Illustrator

Yuri Vinogradov is an artist who has been described as 'a poet of the silence'. His unique and highly recognisable style has received international acclaim. Yuri's work transports the viewer from their everyday reality into the world of inner landscape and imagination. It has been displayed in a variety of settings, from underground cafés and garages of his native Belarus to the trendy art galleries of Germany and Israel. Yuri lives in Minsk, where he was born.

Thank you, kuti, for the sounds that you let in: the animals, the people, the birds. Thank you for letting the drums in!

Thank you, kuti, for showing me how much I can sweat. I sweated more than ever in my whole life!

Thank you, kuti, for defeating me, for putting me on my knees, down on the floor, for making me collapse. I know now that I can do that, that the earth is there to hold me.

Thank you, kuti, for leaving just enough energy for me to dance, even on the toughest day. I want to dance, whatever happens!

In the Rays of Black

A freedomDANCE Book of Darkness

Alex Svoboda

freedom DANCE HOUSE

Printed in Great Britain
by Amazon

52005178R00050